*Wings of Hope*

# Wings
## of
# Hope

A BOOK OF POEMS

*by*

Joan Walsh Anglund

Random House New York

All rights reserved under International and Pan-American
Copyright Conventions. Published in the United States by
Random House, Inc., New York,
and simultaneously in Canada by Random House of
Canada Limited, Toronto.

Library of Congress Cataloging-in-Publication Data
Anglund, Joan Walsh.
Wings of hope : a book of poems / by Joan Walsh Anglund.
— 1st ed.
p.    cm.
ISBN 0-679-40901-7
I. Title.
PS3551.N47W5    1994
811'.54—dc20                                    94-20310

Manufactured in the United States of America
on acid-free paper.
2    4    6    8    9    7    5    3

*for my dear sister*
*Patsy*
*with all my love*

*Wings of Hope*

Hope
     is the whisper
          deep within,
that says
     "Hold on!
     . . . We yet
          may
            win!"

There is
          no Fear
that
     Love
          cannot
                vanquish.

Every spring blossom
              in the garden
is a messenger
              of Hope

     . . . reminding us, again,
that Life
         is ever
              renewing itself!

The soul
        is naked
in solitude,
        that must clothe
                        itself
        in words
            at the
                    arrival
                    of another.

We fail,

   . . . but then

           rise,

   . . . to

      try

        again!

Nothing
    can defeat you,
unless
    *you*
      surrender!

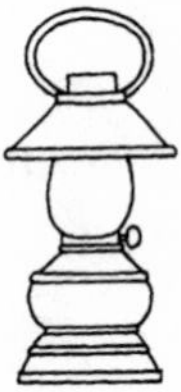

Hope
is the lantern
of the Soul.

Visualize
        the Good
Believe
        the Good
Expect
        the Good
Accept
        the Good

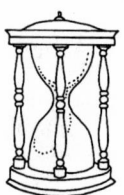

The Love

we give to others

returns,

. . . to bring us

Joy!

Fear
　　　is only
the absence
　　　　　of belief!

Each Heart
must heed
its
own
truth.

The green ferns
        at my feet
quietly unfurl,
   . . . and do not waste
      their brief hour
        in
       worry!

Let my love
          be the chalice
that holds
          Hope's
                    healing elixir
to another's
          thirsting lips.

Acceptance
is
the first step
toward
Peace.

Often

      we are pushed forward
by the need

      to surmount difficulties
. . . as the brook

      is hurried faster

            on its way,
by the very rocks

      that would impede

            its journey.

You cannot
      know
           your strength
  . . . until
        you
           test it.

Even
    as the meadowlark
        in spring,
Hope
    awakens,
        after long despair,
. . . startled,
        to find
            it still can
                sing!

In all of Life's
            greatest trials,
how often
            we find
that our help
            comes
from the most
            unexpected
                  sources!

Let us learn
            to float
. . . as lightly
            as a leaf,
upon
        the varying currents
            of
                life's wide river.

Joy
is the aftermath
of giving!

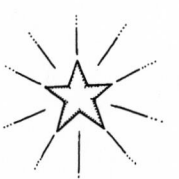

How many
         would have failed,
except
      that Hope
               sustained them
         through the darkness
               . . . until the Light
                        could dawn!

Hour by hour,
thought by thought,
love by love,
we are weaving
our Destiny!

On wings of Hope
            are we lifted,
    above,
        and beyond,
            despair.

*About the Author*

JOAN WALSH ANGLUND, the much-
loved author/illustrator of such cele-
brated titles as *A Friend Is Someone Who
Likes You* and *Love Is a Special Way of
Feeling*, lives with her family in an
eighteenth-century house in Con-
necticut.

Mrs. Anglund was honored by the
Lincoln Academy of Illinois for her
contribution to literature and art. Her
books, which have sold more than
thirty million copies, have been pub-
lished all around the world in over
fourteen languages.